GRIEF IS NOT A PERMANENT CONDITION

FIFTY DEVOTIONALS TO HELP YOU THROUGH THE GRIEVING PROCESS

B . J .   F U N K

WESTBOW
P R E S S®
A DIVISION OF THOMAS NELSON
& ZONDERVAN

WestBow Press books may be ordered through booksellers or by contacting:

WestBow Press
A Division of Thomas Nelson & Zondervan
1663 Liberty Drive
Bloomington, IN 47403
www.westbowpress.com
1 (866) 928-1240

ISBN: 978-1-5127-1741-9 (sc)
ISBN: 978-1-5127-1740-2 (e)

Library of Congress Control Number: 2015917658

Print information available on the last page.

WestBow Press rev. date: 11/04/2015

To Roy, my beloved husband in heaven
And to our five fine sons and their families

Vince and Terri Funk, Jacob, Morgan and Reagan
Deron and Mandy Funk, Brandon and Cortney
Shawn and Mariana Stafford
Chad Smith
Robby and Hollie Funk, Julie and Ellie

CONTENTS

Weeping May Endure for A Night
But Joy Comes in the Morning
Psalm 30:5

At this moment, you are not sure about this verse. The pain of yesterday still has you in its tight grip. The suffering of today has filled you with tears. Nothing seems to make you better. Friends arrive. Family comes around. Food fills your refrigerator. Cards flood your mailbox. You receive each with a heart of gratitude. Yet, how can they understand? Who can know how you really feel when you yourself can't even get in touch with your feelings? All you know is that darkness has fallen in your heart, and things will never be the same.

I offer this short devotional book in hopes that the title will encourage you to hold on. As unbelievable as it sounds to you today, a time will come when you will see the faint break of dawn opening over the horizon of your gray heart. You will sense a joy you thought you had lost. You will---*believe it*---wake up one morning and know for sure that you will make it.

Grief is a process. Be patient with yourself while you are healing. It could take from one and a half to three years to work through your pain. This does not mean that all of this time will be spent in never-ending tears. This means that you need to give yourself permission to take all the time you need, and often that means up to three years. You will smile during this time; you will laugh; you will want to escape and be alone; you will want to be with friends; you will accomplish nothing some days; on other days you will surprise yourself with how much you will get done.

I hope you will take time to read the Scripture located under each title. If that particular day's reading does not apply to you, skip it for now. However, you might find that you will go back again and again to a particular verse and title. All of these teachings did not happen to me, though many did. I have included them because of my encounters with other grieving people

My husband, Roy, died from Chronic Myeloid Leukemia on April 18, 2009. I am writing this devotional book hoping that something from my experience will help and bless you in your experience with grief.

It is our joy and our duty to reach out our hand of encouragement to those following in our footsteps. I hope you will take mine as we journey together through the night of grief, followed eventually by the joy of morning. The statement is true: Grief is *not* a permanent condition.

B.J. Funk
Chula, Georgia
November, 2015

DAY 1

WALKING THE GRIEF ROAD

But you, O God, do see trouble and grief.
—Psalm 10:14

The road called grief has many curves. One day, you might think you are going in a straight line during your grief walk. You get up feeling pretty good, you are able to move a little faster, and you are feeling better about life. But by the next day, you have found hills, sharp curves, and lots of stones and rocks that make you fall down. Later, you begin another stretch of smooth highway, moving awkwardly and slowly just in case a curve comes out of nowhere. You feel encouragement, but then a large crack in the pavement suddenly causes you to fall down and cut your knees. Once you are up, you decide to go back into your home, where the tranquility of being alone sounds better than ever. You decide it will be a long time before you try that again!

Decisions to move forward are sometimes painful. The bed calls out to us to "stay here a little longer," and the security of the familiar urges us not to try anything new. Friends call to invite us over, but you can't go. Not yet. Death moved into your heart, ripping you into threads and boldly claiming someone dear to you. Socializing is the last thing on your mind today.

If you will look, you will hear something that speaks a different voice and sings a different song. *Hope.* Hope walks by you, even though you dare not believe it. Hope moves effortlessly, a whisper of the future in each step. God says through hope, "I have some plans for you. I am not finished with you yet. Hold on. A new day is coming."

Believe in hope, even when you cannot see it or hear it. Believe in God, even when you think He is not watching.

DAY 2

WHAT DO I DO WITH MY ANGER?

To those who sold doves, Jesus said, "Get these out of here!
How dare you turn my Father's house into a market!"
—John 2:16

Prepare yourself for this one truth: very likely—*more than* likely—you will have feelings of anger move in and out from time to time. God gave us every emotion we have, so why do we often feel we need to apologize for being angry over our loved one's death? A huge slice of your heart has been cut out of you. Cuts cause bleeding. You are bleeding inside every day. You might experience anger at the one who died, at those who might have prevented the death, or at those who were a part of causing the death. You might—more than likely—be mad at God.

It is not God's nature to have to explain anything to us. We are not invited to a question-and-answer session with Him. We can do one of two things with our anger. We can let it grow inside, fester into huge sores, keep the anger for years, and realize that eventually this anger could be a factor in our own demise, or we can ask God to help us let it go. It's okay that we experience the anger, talk about it, cry about it, and pitch a fit about it, but only for a season. Eventually, you will want to become healthy again, and that can happen only as you let go of your anger.

When Jesus told the money changers in the temple to get out, He was angry with them! He made a whip out of cords, scattered the coins, and overturned the tables of the money changers. There was a reason for His anger. He called the temple "my Father's house" and was incensed that others did not show the respect the temple deserved.

2

Believers are the new temple of God, the "Father's house" in which Christ dwells. Your temple is a sacred trust from God, and now tables of pain have been set up inside you. One table is named Hurt, another is Bruised, another is named Lonely, another Anger, and yet another is Confused. If these tables remain in your temple very long, they will take over. The sweet presence of the living God cannot dwell where these tables reside. Take the first step today. Ask Jesus to turn over your anger table. Then, one by one, name these tables of pain, and invite Jesus to turn each table over. Sit back in faith's arms, and watch love go to work.

DAY 3

DARK MORNINGS AND DREADFUL NIGHTS

Humbly accept the Word planted in you, which can save you.
—James 1:21

Many days, you will wake up to dark mornings. Many nights will be dreadful. This is normal at first, of course, but if you feel darkness moving in permanently, you will want to remedy that. Do not be afraid of the miracle of an antidepressant to help you. This does not show a spiritual weakness. This shows that you are smart enough to recognize this medical breakthrough as a temporary gift.

Plant the Word inside of you, letting it pour out all over your wounded soul. Find a trusted friend who will listen more and talk less, someone with whom you can vent your anger, and he or she will not condemn you. You do not need someone who tells you how to get through this grief, lecturing you on what you are doing wrong. If you find at least *one friend* who sits and listens while you cry, you will be more blessed than many.

Nothing makes sense right now. You will feel all alone, especially when the last one leaves and you are left with only your thoughts. Look for the sunshine, but when you don't see it, plant a new patch for yourself. Do something that makes you smile. Recognize that others have been where you are, and still others will come after you. Don't make any serious decisions when mornings are dark and nights are dreadful.

Allow yourself to talk to a professional about your depression. Call your pastor and ask for prayer. Start blogging your thoughts. Begin a journal. Make yourself into a whole person again. Lean on the everlasting arms of Jesus. Play Christian music in your home. Find Christian radio stations.

Saturate yourself with Jesus. Soak in Him, rest in Him, delight in Him, and find that when you do, He is delighting, resting, and soaking in you. You are His everything. He must be yours if you are to survive.

DAY 4

TOO NUMB TO FEEL ANYTHING

Because of the Lord's great love, we are not
consumed, for His compassion never fail
Lamentations 3:22

If your faith is based on feelings, you live in a shallow boat tossing around in the sea. If your faith is based on facts, then you are brilliantly alive! Fact: Jesus came. He died. He arose. You are saved if you accept this good news.

Feelings go up and down, as fickle as the waves in the sea, some swelling to monstrous heights while others are so slow we hardly notice. Our faith, however, is based on the facts of the Bible, and those don't always come with a "Hallelujah-Amen-Angel-Chorus!" Check your faith pulse. Do you need an adrenalin shot in the form of great emotion in order for you to have feelings? Or is your faith based on the above-mentioned facts that cause feelings of deep peace, serenity, joy, and harmony with life? Those who have only a "feel good" religion will have the hardest time making it through grief. They keep looking for a "kick," something to make them believe in a new miracle, something to make them shout, "Glory!" Those who have a deep abiding faith in a powerful God will settle down with their Maker in sweet contentment. Nothing life throws at them can toss them into the sea of constant turmoil forever.

The compassion of our Lord is never-ending! He has plenty for you today. If it wasn't for His great love, we would be consumed by this burden called grief. Instead, grief is an antidote to our hurts. It can be a panacea for all our pain if we will sit back and let God do His work.

It is okay if you don't feel anything today. You will. Feelings will come back. *Restored* feelings. Even happy feelings. You will smile again. Even giggle. You are in a life class now. Grief is the classroom and pain is your teacher, but Jesus is your one and only healer. Let Him do what He has been doing for centuries. Allow Him the privilege of healing you. Talk to Him, and let Him help you.

DAY 5

WILL THE TEARS EVER STOP?

Why are you downcast, O my soul?
Why so disturbed within me?
—Psalm 43:5

Tears are a cleansing element that bring to the surface all those deeply painful circumstances in our lives. If you never cry, others will wonder why you display such little emotion concerning one you confessed to love. Even the strongest cry. When Peter realized that he had betrayed Christ and disowned Him, "He went outside and wept bitterly" (Luke 22:62). Jesus *wept* when Lazarus died (John 11:35). You might choose to cry alone, when only God and you are present, or you might choose to cry in the familiarity of a close and trusted friend. Or you might not get to choose. Tears have a way of springing up at moments when we are not expecting them. Crying is often an emotion that bubbles quietly inside like a hidden volcano. A volcano can erupt when you least expect it.

God does not view tears as weakness. When tears interrupt our conversations, we apologize. "I'm sorry. I was not going to do this!" You actually made plans to stifle a gift from God? There are certain tears you just cannot hold back. Allow them. Use them. You never have to apologize for them.

Today your soul is downcast and disturbed, but even grief comes to an end. *Grief is not a permanent condition.* Better days await you. They will be greeted in healthy ways if you do the work that grief requires. Take your time. Let the tears flow. Thank God that your emotions have a safe place to go, a place that allows an outlet through your eyes. Thank God that in His absolutely divine and perfect plan, He gave you tear ducts made especially so your tears can flow. As you cry, think about your Lord, from whom flows something else, something magnificent, something precious. Something called blessings. A familiar doxology sung in many churches has this line: *Praise God from whom all blessings flow.* Let your tears flow, and realize that, as your tears flow, so do His blessings. Look for them today.

DAY 6

The Pain of "How are you?"

Keep me safe, O God, for in you I take refuge
Psalm 16:1

Somewhere, between the days of Jesus and the twenty-first century, "How are you?" crept into our society as our standard greeting. For those going through grief, the question is unbearable. Never mind that the one speaking to you actually does not intend that you answer. It is just the standard, the accepted greeting, and the phrase falls from our lips often unaware. You walk through the checkout counter at the grocery store. The clerk does not even know you, but she asks, as she moves your groceries along, "How are you today?" Emotions inside explode. You cannot really tell anyone exactly how you are! Would the clerk really want to hear that you are grief-stricken, with no hope at the moment that things will improve. You either give back the standard answer, "Fine, thank you. How are you?" or you get out of the store as quickly as you can, hoping no one notices the tears.

No one means any harm. You are experiencing a very deep and private emotional battle, and the last thing you want to do is say, "Fine, thank you!" Instead, you want to say to the clerk, "I hate this moment here at the store with you. I detest that you ask me how I am! I have no good answer to describe the depth of my emotion. Why don't you just deal with groceries and not ask me any questions." Of course, you won't say that. You don't dare say that.

Here's a suggestion. Since that other person has no clue how you really are, spare her the details. Do the same for friends who ask "How are you" when you are in public places where your details would make her/him

10

uncomfortable. They do not mean to make you suffer with this, so don't make them suffer with your response. People are uncomfortable dealing with pain and death. Your simple response of "Thanks for asking. I'm holding on," will give them permission to move out of this conversation comfortably. At other times, in the privacy of a setting with a close friend, tell them how you really are. A good friend has all the time in the world for you.

Unless we adopt "How are you?" "Fine, thank you," as our national motto, you really do not have to explain anything to anyone. You will do yourself a favor, however, to be prepared that this will happen. Appreciate the sincere intent on the part of the other person, while clinging to Psalm 16:1. Inside the temple of you, where Christ lives, *take refuge in Him.* Silently give the question to Jesus, and plan to talk with Him about it later. You don't owe an explanation about anything to anybody.

DAY 7

WHY IS THIS HAPPENING TO ME?

Though He brings grief, He will show compassion,
So great is His unfailing love.
Lamentations 3:32

At some point in your grief, you may think or ask these questions: "Why me? What have I done to deserve this? Am I being punished?" The answer to the first question is "Why not you?"

The answer to the second is "Nothing." And the answer to the third is "Definitely not."

Our world has been on a downward spiral since Adam and Eve disobeyed in the Garden of Eden. None of us can escape the sin-factor that began at that time. That sin-factor includes unexpected and sudden illness, unexpected and sudden car accidents, and unexpected and sudden trauma of any kind. We are all a part of a swirling downfall that will never stop until Jesus comes back. Instead of "Why me?" we might better ask, "Why not me before now? As part of the drowning-in-sin human race, I could have been a victim many, many times before. Thank God I have not!"

No one is exempt from suffering. It is our training ground for warfare with Satan. When we learn that we can do *all things through Christ with His abiding presence,* we then realize that sin, even though it weaves a destructive path, cannot truly touch the part of us that is real. Sin cannot get to our spirit. Sin cannot take away our peace.

It is not quite true to say that you have done nothing to deserve this. Because you were born with the propensity to sin, and because you were born into a sinful environment, full of germs and disease and gravity that controls cars as they career off of a cliff, then you did something by coming to earth in the first place. The day you were born you joined the rest of us in being victim to sufferings none of us asked for. You did not have a choice in being born, and you do not have a choice in suffering.

The simple truth is, however, that you did nothing to deserve what you are going through now. Don't waste your time analyzing your bad decisions, your bad thoughts or your bad actions. In most situations, we cannot take the blame for what has happened. If, however, you feel a direct connection with this pain, take it to Jesus. Ask for forgiveness. Ask for strength to move past this and to come out deeply connected to His heart.

You are not being punished. In John 9:2, the disciples spoke with Jesus about a blind man. "Who sinned? This man or his parents that he was born blind?" Jesus answered, "Neither. This happened so that the work of God might be displayed in his life." In this particular story, the blind man was healed. That has not happened in your situation. There will, however, be some sort of healing if you hand this to Jesus. Lives might be changed. Dissensions among family members could be healed. Hearts of stone might be softened. If you didn't get the big miracle, look for the little ones, and watch the *work of God* being displayed in your life.

DAY 8

BUT, I DON'T WANT MEMORIES!

He gives strength to the weary and
increases the power of the weak.
Isaiah 40:29

You would like the clock to stop. You want to crawl back into the years
before this pain and keep the hands at that place always. Well-meaning
family and friends will say to you, "You have great memories with your
loved one. You must concentrate on that." Would they understand if you
shouted back, "But, I don't want the memories. I want him/her!" Some
days, when sanity moves back into your mind for a few hours, you realize
how absurd that sounds. Most days, you just wish it could be true.

Maybe you cannot look at pictures, yet, or read cards or letters from the
one who left. Probably too soon to travel down memory lane, remembering
certain things that were said or sweet actions taken. As with everything,
you have to do what feels right to you. Everyone handles pain differently.
No one has the right to tell you how to grieve, but loved ones do have the
right to care about your grief progress.

A natural feeling is to wish that you could have gone with that one
you loved. At times there is an intense longing to be in the same room
with your loved one, to hold his hand, to touch her face. Isaiah's passage
adequately describes the inability you have to completely handle life right
now. He also points to the ability God has to handle it for you. You will
get your strength by drawing away into quiet moments with God. Sit

in the same room with Him. Let Him hold your hand. Reach up and symbolically touch His face. He really does know how to give strength to the weary and power to the weak. It's a proven fact. Tell your Savior that you want Him to prove this verse to you. Then, sit quietly by and watch.

DAY 9

I AM NOT SURE I CAN MAKE IT!

When I heard these things, I sat down and wept.
Nehemiah 1:4

Bad news grabs our heart and twist it until it literally almost breaks. As much as we try to be prepared, we are never fully prepared for someone's death. Our mind moves back and forth from acceptance to disbelief. When we hear about it, we sit down and weep. Many times. Maybe many, many times. However, even in news that brings great pain, we will need to make plans. Funeral arrangements have to be made. Friends who stop by need to be welcomed. The funeral home will want pictures to display. Who will provide music? Who will preach? Who are the pallbearers?

Nehemiah wept when he learned that the wall of Jerusalem was broken down and its gates burned. As cup bearer to the King of Persia, he was in a place of prominence, one which afforded this Jewish man to see the king daily. He asked for permission to rebuild the Jerusalem wall, and it was granted.

Nehemiah made 'an which included prayer first and organization
se— ... zy, the walls of Jerusalem were rebuilt! When
to be made, often we will begin planning, but
to heal you, and He is amazing with a plan!
been planned out before He carried it through
'rt in this.

have been torn down. You are hurting and
'ou want to build them back, but you don't
'annot make it. Many days you don't want

to even try. But, here's a plan that works: Pray and then organize. You can do it. Give God a chance to show you that, like Nehemiah, you can build again. Still your mind long enough to know that you need prayer focus before organizational focus. It will save you a lot of mistakes.

DAY 10

FIGHTING THE BONDAGE OF "IF ONLY"

"If you had been here, my brother would not have died."
John 11:21

"If only" will weave in and out of your head many times before you are able to put it to rest. Even then, "if only" will come at times when you least expect it. "If only he had not left upset" "If only I had done more for her," "If only they had not left an hour later," "If only I had noticed the early signs of his illness." "If only" will come to the innocent and the guilty, but in either case, it does no good to go there. We cannot change what happened. We will either live the rest of our lives in bondage over what happened, or we will let it go. It takes God's grace and mercy to let it go.

Martha and Mary both approached Jesus with "If only," after their brother, Lazarus, died. In this case, Jesus purposefully was not there with them. He planned to use Lazarus' death as an opportunity to display the power of God. Perhaps He is planning to use your particular situation with death as an opportunity to display the power of God.

Death is an opportunity for the enemy to bring confusion into our already upset lives. Satan loves to throw guilt on us, and at times of loss, we are particularly vulnerable to his lies. Because we all want to do our best for those we love, we easily receive guilt and blame. Jesus does not want you to go the rest of your life blaming yourself for someone's death. Even if you were the "other car" in a terrible accident that was your fault, *you do not have the power to take away someone's life*. Only God has that power. Ecclesiastes reminds us that there is a time to be born and a time to die (Ecclesiastes 3:2a)

Ultimately, you and I don't have anything to do with that timing. The secret to our peace is to accept God's timing-- to recognize it, receive it, and not resent it.

No one can calm you, guide you, or help you like Jesus. Tell Him how you feel, and allow Him to bear your burden.

DAY 11

NEEDING TO BE ALONE

When Jesus heard what had happened (John the Baptist's death),
He withdrew by boat privately to a solitary place.
Matthew 14:13

Jesus gives us a model of what to do when someone we love has died. His cousin, John the Baptist, had been beheaded, and John's disciples came to tell Jesus. Jesus got in a boat and moved away from the crowd. Our Lord must have felt the need to be alone, to sit quietly this news.

Sometime, you might feel the need to draw away from everyone, to sit and think, or to sit and pray. Solitude has its purposes. During quiet moments away from the crowd, you can gain renewed strength to handle what has happened. It is quite okay to draw away. Jesus did.

Family and friends are eager for you to "move on," and they might want to speed up your recovery. Give yourself permission to handle your grief in the way that suits you. You will be glad that you took your time. When you are able, move back into some of the activities you used to enjoy. Baby steps will eventually get you to the same place that giant leaps will, though it will take a little longer. Take all the time you need to nourish all of your heart and soul wounds.

Just as a physical wound's healing cannot be rushed, neither can an emotional wound. In truth, heart-wounds take longer, for there is no salve, no pill, no IV drip and no operation that can make this wound well.

No matter how busy your day, withdraw to a solitary place, either in a physical setting or in your heart, where private moments with Jesus become the medicine you need for your soul.

WHERE WAS GOD WHEN THIS HAPPENED?

The God of Israel Neither Slumbers or Sleeps.
Psalm 121:4

Because we have no one else to blame, we often put the blame on God. After all, He is God! Could He not have prevented what happened to our loved one? Could He not have stopped this sadness? Did He close His eyes and turn away? Does He even care?

You have heard someone say, "This is my business! Stay out of my business!" God says that to us a little differently—in a grace-filled way-- in Isaiah 46: 9, as He reminds us who is in charge: "I am God, and there is no other. I am God, and there is none like me."

Everything that happens is God's business, and not ours. We are His creation. He is the creator! Psalm 121:4 tells us that God does not go to sleep. He is always watching over us. On the other hand, 1 Peter 5:8-9 reminds us that "Your enemy the devil prowls around, like a roaring lion looking for someone to devour. Resist him, standing firm in the faith, because you know that your brothers throughout the world are undergoing the same kind of suffering." Satan prowls, but God neither slumbers or sleeps. He is always watching over us, often protecting us and preventing a tragedy.

Suffering is universal. There is nothing in the Word that tells us those of us who go to church will never suffer. There is no verse that tells us that believers are immune from the tactics of the evil one. There are only two chapters in the whole Bible that are not infected with the result of Adam and Eve's sin: Genesis, chapter 1 and 2. Look at the next chapter, Genesis, chapter 3. The very first words read like this: "Now, the serpent was more crafty than any of the wild animals the Lord God had made." There you have it. Satan entered a snake, and Adam and Eve listened to him instead of God. *Thus, the fall of man and the beginning of the infection of sin. Every person who came after those first two chapters would be born into the sin problem. That includes you and me.*

This does not only mean the sin problem which sways our bad choices, places temptation on a silver platter before us, and causes heartache and strife in families and among friends. This includes the sin problem that affects our bodies with cancer, our minds with Alzheimer's, and might place us in the middle of a wreck, or as the recipient of another's random gunfire. This is not to say that sin in you made those things happen, but that sin *in the world is the reason they happened.* Sin is the problem, and sin encompasses everything that brings hurt, pain, disease, and grief.

God is a God of love. He does not wish any of these heartaches on His children. But, starting in Genesis, chapter three, the free will of man to make choices brought the downward spiral of man. That's exactly why we need a Savior. Do we have the power through Jesus to overcome our temptations? Yes. We claim our body as His Temple, and ask Him to reign, giving us strength against the evil one. But until the end of time when Satan is thrown into the lake of fire, Satan will prowl, and we will struggle with sin's effects. We will not be free of disease or natural disaster until Jesus comes.

Where was God when this happened to you? Where He always is … watching over you, protecting you, loving you, hurting with you, and giving you hour by hour strength to make it, whatever you are facing.

DAY 13

HOW LONG WILL I KEEP CRYING?

I am worn out from groaning. All night long
I flood my bed with weeping and drench my couch with tears.
Psalm 6:6

David, mighty warrior and King of Israel ... the same David who earlier in his life slew a giant with a rock and a sling shot ... this same David is *worn out* from crying. He does not say he is worn out from the battle, or worn out from being a leader. He is *worn out* from crying! His couch is drenched with his tears. He floods his bed all night long. We do not know the cause of David's pain in psalm 6:6, but we do know that David is being honest with God as he confesses his human weakness

You can be honest with God, too. He knows how you feel, so no need in trying to hide your feelings from Him. In verse 9 of this same psalm, David lets us know that he is one hundred percent sure that God has heard his prayer: " ...for the Lord has heard my weeping."

Refuse to accept the lie Satan wants you to believe, that God is a mean and unkind ogre, delighting in throwing out pain to his children. It is not true! God grieves with us. He recognizes our sin problem, and He hurts over the pain we have. His Son Jesus chose to enter this world of sin to experience what you and I face. God knows about pain, not just the pain of walking over rocks, scraping His knees, or maybe hurting his finger in the carpenter's shop. He also knows the intense pain of a whip on His body and nails in His wrists. He knows the pain of a spear thrust in His side, the pain of a body nailed in a non-changeable position on a cross, with no chance of relief. He knows the pain of feeling weak and losing His life as His blood is spilled out.

Does God understand your pain? Yes, He does. Hebrews 4:15 reminds us "For we do not have a high priest who is unable to sympathize with our weakness, but we have one (Jesus!) who has been tempted in every way, just as we are—yet without sin."

Psalm 30: 5b reminds us that, "weeping may endure for a night, but JOY comes in the morning." Along with the night, there is darkness and loss of hope. We cannot see to find our way. With the morning, however, comes sunshine, light, new opportunities and fresh hope.

How long will you keep crying? However long it takes. Welcome the brief interruptions of hope until a new and longer season comes, a season of morning and new possibilities. Allow yourself to be surprised by God's joy.

DAY 14

UNBEARABLE LONELINESS

The Lord is my strength and my shield;
My heart trusts in Him, and I am helped.
Psalm 28:7

You could be all by yourself now, and the loneliness is unbearable. Or, you might be with a lot of family every day, and yet, the loneliness is still unbearable. A silent room points to a missing part of your life. An empty house shouts a reminder that someone will never walk into your room again. There is an absent presence, a huge void, an unbearable sense of loss that never leaves. Your loved one may not have occupied the same home you do, but he/she occupied a huge space in your heart. That heart-wound calls out daily for a presence that is no longer here. Deep grief tugs at our sanity. Heavy hurts close in on us like a cage.

Welcomed familiar sounds invade your space. An air conditioner clicks on, the ice-maker drops ice, and the drier buzzes. You find comfort in those things that have not changed. The phone rings, and you wish it would ring again. The wind outside your window blows an intimate assurance that, even though your world has stopped, some things have not. People at the grocery store are doing "business as usual," and it helps to know that, for some, life goes on. Maybe it will one day for you.

At first, you avoid places the two of you knew together. You walk out when a certain song comes on the radio. You lie awake until early hours of the morning, wondering if you will ever be able to know a day of peace. Well-meaning family and friends come around, wanting to help. You are glad. You know that you need them. But, at the end of the day, it is still just you, without that person. Every evening you have to deal with the pain of loss, and every morning brings a new reminder. Will you ever be able to live again?

Each day brings a new opportunity to trust in the Lord and to find your strength in Him. If you were not able to yesterday, then start over again today. Tell Him how hard this is for you. Cry and mourn as you release your loneliness to Him. He is the only One who can really help you. Depend on Him to bring you out of darkness into His marvelous light.

How will you know when it happens? One day you will hear a bird singing and wonder why you had not heard that bird before. Truth is, she was always singing. You just could not hear the song.

When you start hearing the song, your healing has begun.

DAY 15

I FEEL OUT OF CONTROL!

Jesus looked at them and said, "With man this is
impossible, but with God all things are possible."
Matthew 19:26

The tears, the anger, the loneliness all join together to remind us that we
cannot control the situation we are in. We used to feel somewhat in control
of things. Now, we feel as if we are on a merry-go-round that could easily
sling us off at any minute. We don't have access to the switch to stop the
constant round and round, the never-ending organ music that plays the
same depressing song over and over as we ride. We are dizzy, just as much
from the consistency of the merry-go-round as we are from the reality that
this might never end. Will we ever be able to make decisions again? Will
we ever be able to feel comfortable doing those things the other person did
for us? Our head spins with the questions that play over and over: "Why
did this happen to me? How can I ever handle those things I have never
had to handle before?" Will I ever feel "in control" again?"

Jesus whispers into your spirit today the same thoughts He whispered
to those who have faced tragedy before us. "No, not by yourself. Why don't
you hand it all over to me, and watch what I can do for you." That is the
secret. Hand the key of your heart over to Jesus. He will then use His key
to open doors no one else can open.

Isaiah 45:7 says, "I form the light and create darkness. I bring prosperity
and create disaster. I, the Lord, do all these things."

We cannot possibly understand this verse, so we read it, and then
ask for faith. The point is that God has not left us to chance. He may

allow darkness or light to enter our lives, but all the while, He is carefully watching us, hoping that this will be the chance He has been waiting for. What chance is that? The chance for Him to show you how precious you are to Him, and that with Him, all things are indeed possible. A popular song says, "He will make a way where there seems to be no way."

Yes, even for you.

DAY 16

EVERY STEP FEELS HEAVY

"If only my anguish could be weighed and all my misery be placed
on the scales. It would surely outweigh the sand of the seas."
Job 6: 2-3a

The weight of grief is hard to describe. You are sure that no one has experienced it the same way you have. For if they had, surely they would not have survived. You don't think you will either.

Every step hurts. Every move feels awkward. You lose your sense of real verses unreal. This just cannot be happening! How could it? Your shoulders slope down under the weight of this burden, and your heart pounds so loudly you are sure everyone can hear. Do tears make a sound as they move into your eyes and down your cheeks? They do for you.

You never knew before the origin of your tears, but now you know. They start in your feet, moving up past every muscle, tissue and organ and rapidly gathering all the hurts. Soon, there is a long chain of tears moving toward your eyes. When they finally flow out, you are stunned at the rush of liquid, the strong waterfall of pain you have held in. Let them flow. Let your tears do what only tears can do.

Job gives a painfully adequate description of sorrow. He tells in believable imagery that the weight of his anguish outweighs all the sands of the sea. Job's burden of loss was more than he could bear. Job lost all that he had. He battles with life's circumstances, trying to understand "why?"

In the end, after 42 chapters of questioning and listening to his friends, he realized that he was not meant to know the reasons. Job had to face life without the answers and explanations. We do too. The only thing we can know for sure is that the only way we can get through our days and nights is by trusting God. We won't get the answers, but we will get a deeper and more abiding sense of God's presence as we place our heaviness into His strong and capable hands.

DAY 17

DESPAIR AND DEFEAT

With God we will gain the victory, and He
will trample down our enemies.
Psalm 60:12

You will not always feel this way. Better days and nights are on their way. The despair you feel today will not stay. Our God is a God of victory, not defeat. He wants to go before you to make things easier. Let Him. Ask Him to replace your despair with new hope and your defeat with new faith. Don't remain in the company of those who speak of despair as if it will be a life-long problem. Choose not to be around those whose negative talk makes you feel that life's hurt has defeated you. Turn away from those who cannot move past pain and into wholeness. The company you choose matters.

Choose, instead, those whose lives are guided by a Divine hand, whose daily hope rests in the leadership of our great and wonderful Father God. Seek counsel from a wise mentor, someone who has been in your shoes, but their life proves that you will be able to overcome, as they have. Stay in the Word of God. Make it your daily life-line to God. Without your intimate conversations with your Lord, you will not be able to move forward. This … the death of someone you love … will not fade away like a perfume that fills the air for a moment, and then gradually goes away. Death stays in the air like tons of hot black tar pressing down on you wherever you go. It is relentless in its effort to keep black clouds hanging.

On the other hand, resurrection is quite different. Gradually, you will realize that the sting of death is hurting less and less. It is being replaced with glorious resurrection power. Christ overcame death. He had victory over death and the grave. Until you move away from death to a conscious awareness of resurrection, you will dwell inside darkness. Someone's life has been lost. Don't lose yourself in their death, too. If a believer, then your loved one has been resurrected to live in heaven. You can be resurrected out of the depth of gloom and despair.

Jesus has a wrapped gift to hand you. Reach up and take it. It is the gift called *Perfect Peace in the Midst of the Storm*. The gift has your name on it, but you cannot receive it unless you open it.

Do yourself a favor. Open God's gift to you. Let perfect peace rest all over you today. The struggle will never leave under your own efforts. He is your Perfect Peace.

DAY 18

FINDING IT HARD TO TRUST GOD

Trust in the Lord with all your heart, and lean
not on your own understanding.
Proverbs 3:5

When your emotions are shattered, and you feel you cannot take one more day of pain, God reminds us that we were never meant to do this by ourselves. People let us down. Our trust cannot be in men or women, well-intentioned as they might be. Friends and family can be wonderful, but there is only just so much they can do. Our trust must eventually find its way back to our Creator, God. He is the only One who knows the beginning from the end in our particular situation. He is the only One you can truly count on. Thankfully, He might send others who can give good counsel. He might place the perfect book in your path. He is good at sending those who have been where you are. For all of these things, you will give thanks. However, nothing can satisfy you like Jesus. No shoulder is as strong as His. No heart beats perfectly with yours as does His. No one loves you more than He does.

There are two teachings in this verse in Proverbs. First, we are to trust in the Lord. Secondly, we are to lean not on our own understanding. Trusting and Leaning. *Impossible on our own.* With God, though, all things are possible. Talk to God about how hard it is for you to trust Him again. After all, He did not save your loved one from death, even though you prayed often. At times like this, God reminds us, as He did Job, with questions like these: "*Who* has the wisdom to count the clouds? *Who* can tip over the water jars of the heavens when the dust becomes hard and the clods of earth stick together?" (Job 38: 38)

In the next chapter, God asks Job, "Does the hawk take flight *by your wisdom* and spread his wings toward the south? Does the eagle soar *at your command* and build his nest on high?" (Job 39: 26-27) In chapter 40, Job seems to have caught on when he says to God, "I am unworthy---how can I repay You. I put my hand over my mouth." (Job 40:4) It seems the Almighty "puts Job in his place," with these questions. Job recognizes how small he is and how great God is. Our trust can never be in our selves ... for we have no power ... but only in our Sovereign God.

The second part of this Scripture tells us not to lean on what we know or don't know. In fact, if we lean on our own understanding, we will never find our proper healing. We will be leaning on what is perishable, what is fleeting, what is second-best. Make yourself start the practice of leaning on Jesus, not on anyone or anything else. How do you do that?

You just do. You decide that you will, and then you allow God to do what He does best, like tipping water jars out of heaven.

DAY 19

I'M SCARED OF THE FUTURE WITHOUT HER/HIM

The Lord is my light and my salvation--whom shall I fear?
The Lord is the stronghold of my life--of whom shall I be afraid?
Psalm 27

Electric lights go out. The light of the sun fades when night comes. A flashlight can only shine in a certain direction and with a limited stream. Candles burn out. Only the Lord's light stays. Only the light from God can give us what we need, and His light never goes out. Psalm 105 reminds us that "Thy Word is a lamp unto my feet and a light unto my path." Everywhere you step, God's Word shines before you, dispelling the darkness. Every path you take is illumined by God's Word! His light shines on you with guidance each morning, and blankets you at night with a fresh glow of solid advice. Your mind might be saying to you right now, "Then, why don't I hear it? Why don't I see it? Why don't I recognize that divine lamp and light?"

In everything we do to gain our healing after a death, we have to be purposeful and intentional. Purpose in your heart to see the Lord's light. Purpose to catch His light as you walk each new path. Decide that you will do whatever it takes to make it. At the top of your "make it" list, the Word of God beckons you to "take and read." If you don't read God's word, hear God's word and believe God's word then the above verse will read for you, "*If only* I would read the Word … then the Lord would be my light and my salvation. I will not fear. *If only* I will claim Him as the stronghold of my life … then I will not be afraid of anyone or anything." Be intentional.

35

Put other things aside--the cares of the world, the obligations of your job in order to have some priority time with your Lord.

As you begin to put yourself anew each morning under the Lord's lamp, you will lose your fear of the future. You will gain a strong determination, fed by reading God's Word, that you will not be defeated by this loss. You will continue to live, and you will live abundantly. It will happen.

Today, breathe in the Lamb of God and the Light of the world, and watch your fears begin to vanish.

DAY 20

MY LOVED ONE DID NOT DESERVE THIS

> He causes His sun to rise on the evil and the good, and
> sends rain on the righteous and the unrighteous.
> Matthew 5:45

No one deserves cancer or car accidents or gun shots. No child deserves to be born missing a chromosome, thus being handicapped all of his/her life. No one deserves to die at the hand of a maniac or a person so doped up that he does not even know what he is doing. No one deserves to be killed by a drunk driver. No one. We all agree. Yet, it happens. Where pain, heartache and death are concerned … well, what can happen to one can surely happen to another.

What we want to believe is that if someone is a Christian, then none of the really bad things happen to them. Then, we look around and realize that statement is false. Bad things *do* happen to Christians. Christians are as prone to be the recipient of crimes, drunk drivers and cancer as anyone. God allows His sun to rise on those who are evil and also on those who are not evil. When He sends the rain, He causes the rain to fall on those who are not evil and those who are evil.

Life is not about what we deserve. Life is about the way we handle whatever happens to us, those things we deserve and things we don't. Life is not about the darts that burst our bubbles, but what we do with the remaining bubbles. Life is not about the calamities that pulled the wind out from under our boat, but how long it took us to get the sails going again. Life is not about how many tears we cried, but how long it took us

37

to find the tissues. Life is not about falling down. It is about how many times we tried to get back up.

It is natural to grieve over the unfairness of what happened. Surely, our merciful and compassionate God understands our sorrow. We must continue giving our sorrow over to God, every day, over and over again, until one day the pain isn't quite as bad.

Life is not about how well we move through the stages of grief; it's about what we do during the quiet time between each stage and the next. It's about what we do with the silences when nobody is watching.

DAY 21

WHY CAN'T I THINK STRAIGHT ANYMORE?

Do not be conformed any longer to the pattern of this world,
but be transformed by the renewing of your mind.
Romans 12:2

New challenges seem to rise every day. You are bombarded with others wanting you to get better. Many try to tell you how you "ought" to be getting through this. Even people you hardly know seem to think they are experts in your recovery. A lot of voices are calling out to you. You want to find a remote hide-a-way, turn off your phone, and not talk to anybody for the next month! You get irritated easily. You want to put a sign on you that reads, "Do I look like I need your opinion?"

Despite what you might feel right now, most are not purposefully trying to confuse you or boss you. Before you strike back, slow down and take a deep breath. Don't say something that you will need to apologize for later. Right now, your mind is justifiably on overload. It's a good time to drink in some of God's Scripture.

Romans 12:2 reminds us not to be conformed to the pattern of the world. The world out there has no clue of God's Word and how Christians seek to gain insights through it. The world has its mind on other things, like how to get rich, how to have what your neighbor has or how to win a jackpot full of money. The rest of Romans 12:2 reminds us that we can be transformed as we renew our mind. What does that mean?

Because of the onslaught of garbage that comes into our minds in our trash-infiltrated world, we need to constantly try to flush out the efforts of Satan. You are prey to him simply because you woke up this morning.

He dominates the air waves and the magazines stacked in our stores. Unfortunately, our children are targeted by him, and painful revelations of mistreatment and abuse fall on them. The richness of God's word, however, offers the panacea for all of our hurts. We are not to be conformed, but transformed. You cannot think straight because your mind is cluttered with details and information overload.

Determine today to slow down and drink from the fountain of life. Allow His living water to flow into your brain, sprinkling freshness into your tiredness and new life into your broken dreams. You can only find this help in one way. Consciously let go of the clutter and ask Jesus to take you where He desires. Join Him in an adventure of love. Let Him pull His thread of life through your brokenness, as He mends you back to wholeness. You might be giving alcohol and pills a chance. Why not give Jesus a chance, too. He's good at it. He's done it before. He can do it for you

DAY 22

NEEDING A FRIEND

If one falls down, his friend can help him up.
But pity the man who falls and has no one to help him up.
Ecclesiastes 4: 10

Sometimes we are hit anew with the way things were, and the way they are now. When family is out of town and good friends are busy with their own families, we feel out of place. *Just where do I fit in?* Of course, your friends and family insist that they want you to go out with them, to tag along with their outings. It's hard. It's not easy being the "extra" at restaurants or movies. You might be uncomfortable being in groups in which your loved one once was a part. Sometimes, it's just easier to stay by yourself than to make the effort.

If you are falling down emotionally, Ecclesiastes 4:10 reminds you that you are blessed if you have one friend to help you up. We all need someone to walk the road with us, to listen to our pain, to hear our cries, and to help us up when we are falling. Pain fulfills a vital part of its purpose when it enables those who have walked where you walk now, to put out their hand and heart to you. Later, you will be able to do the same for someone else.

A popular song of yesteryear was "You've got a friend" by Carole King. Fortunate is the man or woman who can know for sure that the friend mentioned in this song would indeed be there.

"You just call out my name. And you know wherever I am. I'll come running to see you again. Winter, spring, summer or fall. All you have to do is call. And I'll be there, You've got a friend.'"

There is another friend, however, that you can always count on ... for sure!! Proverbs 18: 24 speaks of "a friend who sticks closer than a brother." That would be the Lord Jesus Christ! You may wander all around in your heart, chasing after dreams, making new decisions, or just trying to live your life the best you can, and all the while, there is one who never leaves. Others may leave. Jesus does not.

If you are struggling with feeling "left out" of things, talk to Jesus about your need. Spend some alone time with Him in prayer and in reading His love book to you, the Holy Word of God. If you read it, *really really* read this book, you will know for certain that you would be able to give up all other cherished friendships, but you must have this one. Jesus is the BBF (Best Friend Forever) you can ever have.

DAY 23

FEELING HOLLOW INSIDE

Fear and trembling seized me and made all my bones shake
Job 4:14

You remember something of how it used to feel to be alive, but right now you can't find that feeling. You recall something of feeling happy, but that feeling has left. You look at pictures of yourself in years past, and you looked happy. You believe that there is such a thing as happiness, and you pray that one day happiness will come back. Until it does, what do you do?

Nights are worse. Sometimes, you feel your bones are shaking as fear and trembling overtake you. How can you find life again?

Look around. Find someone who has walked in your shoes and is still breathing. Talk to that person. Find out how they did it. Determine that if they can, you can, too. It actually helps to know that others who have had the same tragedy happen to them are moving on with life. They give you hope that you, too, will one day move on. And, you will.

You remember what it felt like to thrill with the beginning of each new day. You had so much to live for, so much joy for which to be thankful. Now, the thrill is gone and joy seems a thing in your distant past. Will you ever find the thrill of living again? Is joy gone forever?

Sometimes, because we do not want to burden others, we tell them we are doing "just fine." In fact, sometime we say we are "great" when we really aren't

Grief is hard work. It doesn't happen in one day, one week or one month. Remember to give yourself one and a half to three years of working through your pain. That does not mean you will be grief-stricken to the

43

point of inability to live during that time. It simply means that you are to be patient with yourself for that long. If, however, you lived with your loved one's sickness for a long time, you likely did a good bit of your grieving while he/she was alive.

You will find yourself smiling, even laughing some as this time period progresses. You will heal the best if you grieve the best.

A popular expression of excitement or disappointment once was "Good grief!" Then, a book on grieving was written with that name. It's really true. *Grief is good.* We need to allow grief to do its work in us so that we can continue doing God's work for Him.

DAY 24

BUT, I DEPENDED ON HIM/HER

We were under great pressure, far beyond our ability to endure, so that we despaired even of life. Indeed, in our hearts we felt the sentence of death. But this happened that we might not rely on ourselves, but on God.
2 Corinthians 1: 8b-9

One of the most difficult parts of being without that one you loved is to face each new day learning how to unlearn. In fact, each day carries within it the unraveling of what used to be. We struggle with the concept that things are not as they once were. You might have to make decisions someone else always made, but that someone is no longer here. You may have a physical handicap, and that person who took care of you is no longer here. Whatever your situation, know that there are others ... many others ... in the same situation as you are. There any many who are floundering in the ocean of "What do I do with myself now?"

When Paul was writing this second letter to the Corinthian church, he believed he and his companions were about to die because of their faith. He did not, however, express fear in this letter. He expressed complete faith in the prayers of the believers and in God's ability to deliver them.

We could learn from Paul. Throughout our lives, God allows certain obstacles or roadblocks so that we can grow to depend on Him, and not on anyone else or on ourselves. These difficulties strengthen us for the journey of life. Your loved one never chose to be a part of this lesson for you, but then, none of us has choices in these matters.

One of the hardest lessons we have to learn is that he/she is not coming back. You are on the right track in your healing when you finally stop looking.

DAY 25

WORKING THROUGH THE FIRST STAGE OF GRIEF
SHOCK AND DENIAL

O Lord, I call to you; come quickly to me
Hear my voice when I call to you.
Psalm 141:1

The phone rang and you could not believe the words on the other end. Or, someone knocked at your door to tell you the news. Fear seized you as you listened. Or, maybe you were the one who found her.

There is no shock that can match that of a sudden, unexpected death. No one can talk you through it or walk you through it. Denial jumps in and out of truth, seeking to claim that this never really happened. Denial tries to be your friend by keeping the truth at bay and helping you to avoid the pain. It is a grand and merciful gesture that will have to be replaced eventually.

Shock keeps your whole body in a state of deep and terrifying torture. You have never known such misery and agony. Surely, you will wake up tomorrow and find out it isn't so. But, a tomorrow like that never comes. Shock wants to be your friend by providing emotional protection from your being overwhelmed all at once. It, too, is a grand and merciful gesture that cannot forever remain.

This first stage will last longer than you expected. Months down the road, when you are feeling better, a morning will come when, though you are starting to move on, shock and denial will come for a visit. They won't stay, and by that time, their visits won't paralyze you as they once did. Shock and denial serve you by helping you to move gradually into the next stages of the tragedy.

You might not be able to eat. Or, you might start eating too much. You might close yourself up in your home. When we don't know what to do with what life has handed us, we *eat or retreat*. Fortunately, this stage will not last.

Even though stages loop in and out of each other, and there is no easy progression from one stage to the next, they can be a guide of what to expect. Still, each person's experience is different.

Give God permission to move with you through the unbelievable pain that life has handed you. He is the only medicine that can help you with this. Listen for His voice. He wants to hold you through this stage and love you as you enter the next one. Down in the bottom of your heart, you are praying even as you cry. "Lord, come quickly to me. Please hear my voice." You will find that He always does.

DAY 26

THE SECOND STAGE OF GRIEF
PAIN AND GUILT

Let us draw near to God with a sincere heart in full
assurance of faith, having our hearts sprinkled
to cleanse us from a guilty conscience, and having
our bodies washed with pure water.
Hebrews 10: 22

Your heart hurts. Your legs and arms hurt. Your face hurts. Nothing feels
normal right now. Mixed with the physical and emotional pain is the guilt
you place on yourself. Why didn't you spend more time with this loved
one? How could you have known that your time was so limited? What
could you have done differently?

What about the last conversation you had? Was it happy and loving?
Or, was it riddled with accusations? Could you have been kinder, spoken
less harshly? What things do you wish you could say now?

The best we can do with these questions is to *let them go*. Time cannot
be packaged and mailed back to you. Words spoken in permanent ink
cannot be erased from a chalkboard. Decisions can not be swallowed. It
is what it is.

Nobody, however, expects you to live the remainder of your life
suffering from what wasn't, what could have been, what happened, or
what did not happen. God alone can sprinkle our hearts with guilt-freeing
salve. He rubs it into the most tender places and knows that He will see
faith-producing results eventually.

It is important to experience your pain fully, rather than masking it under a pretense that life is great. Others won't understand. Don't even expect them to. They have not walked in your shoes. They might even say some hurtful things, thinking they are speaking truth that you need to hear. Don't argue with them. Love them. Then, ask Jesus to continue ridding your heart of a guilty conscience. Misplaced guilt will do no good. It will only drive you into depression or to a mind-altering drug addiction. Make sure that you go to bed with Jesus on your lips and wake up with Him the same way.

This is truth: *there is no other way to make it except through a personal, redeeming, and saving relationship with Jesus Christ!*

DAY 27

THE THIRD STAGE OF GRIEF
ANGER AND BARGAINING

Surely, God, you have worn me out! You have
devastated my entire household!
Job 16:7

Anger claws your heart, pounding you with every beat. You cry out that you don't deserve this, that you never did anything so wrong for this to happen! Sometimes you even scream at God, "Am I this bad? Am I so bad that you had to hurt me like this? What have I done?"

Job expresses his deep pain by telling God that "You have worn me out!" The inner boxing match between you and God or you and pain or you and life has become too deep. You are not sure you can survive much longer. You have been knocked out in the ring, and the referee is counting down your fate.

In this stage, you may blame someone else. You center your anger on them day and night. You cannot be expected to be rational while you are this angry. Like Job, you can be honest with God. Tell Him how you feel. He's big enough to take your anger. He's gracious enough to love you even through your anger.

You might bargain. "If you will make him well, bring him back, change the course of this dreaded disease, stop the process called death, then I will obey you always … never take another drink … give up gambling … start going to church … .tithe."

Bargaining with God has never worked. He is the One who sets the rules, provides the resources, and plans our present and future. Rid your anger by writing out your thoughts or speaking to someone you trust. Find a physical activity through which your anger can find release. Let this stage have its way with you, not because you have the right, but because you must.

Imagine God putting His arms around you, comforting you even as anger takes you to depths you never imagined. Psalm 139 reminds us that there is nowhere we can go but that God goes there with us. "If I go up to the heavens, you are there; if I make my bed in the depths, you are there."

You can never sink so low that His love is not higher.

DAY 28

THE FOURTH STAGE OF GRIEF
DEPRESSION, REFLECTION AND LONELINESS

As fish are caught in a cruel net, or birds are taken in a snare,
So men are trapped by evil times that fall unexpectedly upon them.
Ecclesiastes 9: 12

Do not think that you can get through grief without an occasional, or more than occasional, time of depression. It is normal. Depression suffocates. It robs us of life. Depression whispers cruel things to us at night like, "You should be further along than this by now!" or "You aren't the dedicated Christian you thought you were! Don't you wonder what people are saying about your sad countenance?"

Depression can make us paranoid. We think everybody is watching us, evaluating us and trying to decide how to fix us! We might start thinking too much, asking ourselves too many questions and blaming ourselves again. Well-intentioned family members tell us that "so and so" was out and moving back into her life much sooner! We wonder what is wrong with us?

The truth is that nothing anybody can say will help you feel any better right now. They want to. They try to. But, they just cannot. The best thing anyone can do for you is to *back away* from evaluating you and *move forward* by loving and supporting you.

Just when you think the loneliness has stopped its cruel game of pain, a new avalanche of hurt falls in your lap. Maybe someone said something that upset you. Or, maybe they didn't, but your thoughts focus on what you don't have anymore, and that causes the loneliness to spiral.

Solomon concluded that we are trapped by evil times that fall unexpectedly. He compares our trappings to cruel nets that catch fish and to birds that get caught in a snare. Is it true that we are simply players on a game board, subject to evil trappings that fall unexpectedly? Yes and no. As believers, we know that this world is not just "doing its thing," dangling alone in space, completely disassociated from God's will. At the same time, we also know that evil trappings are true, that innocent victims have cruel tragedies occur in their lives just because they woke up one morning. In a mysterious unexplainable way, the good are often hurt and the bad often go free. Still, our faith claims that God is in control.

The only way I know how to explain this comes from my personal experience over Roy's death from leukemia. I believe that the day Roy died, he stepped into Paradise. I believe that God was not caught unaware. I do not think God looked up from His throne and said, "Roy! I was not expecting *you* today!" Did God cause Roy's death from leukemia? I don't believe He did. Did God know about Roy's death? I believe He did.

I wish this was clearer for you and for me. Some things I learned to file under "don't completely understand, but trust God anyway." Be patient with yourself while you come to the same conclusion. You can go mad trying to figure it out.

This is a time when faith in God—and only that-- becomes your right arm and carries you through each day.

DAY 29

THE FIFTH STAGE OF GRIEF
THE UPWARD TURN

When I was in great need, He saved me
Psalm 117: 6b

At some point in your journey, a beautiful, sweet melody begins to softly drown out all of the other voices within. You cannot put a time or place on the moment you first heard this melody. You were not aware of anything any different. It sort of trickled into your soul with a whisper and then left, promising to come back later. You grabbed it, but it insisted, "Let me go. I will be back!"

A song from my youth went like this: *In my heart there rings a melody, there rings a melody with heaven's harmony; In my heart there rings a melody, there rings a melody of love."* *

That's it! That's the new sound you are hearing. Love's song of *hope and peace* has finally landed on the soil of your heart, begging to be heard. It's not that you denied its entrance. It's just that you weren't ready for it until now. You had to go through all the other stages before you finally began to realize that love truly does make a difference. God's love.

There will be days when you long for the melody, but it does not come, its song dormant amid the eruptions of other voices within. You will jump back and forth, forth and back, in these stages of grief, thinking for sure that one is over when suddenly it comes back, standing tall and proud as if its voice has won the battle for your soul. Don't believe it! Grief stages will play hide-and-go-seek with each other—one hiding as the other seeks to be found---until at last the sounds of grief are a distant echo. Even though you cannot pinpoint the exact moment, you can pinpoint the immeasurably wonderful feeling that comes when you finally feel that "upward turn."

The melody will come back. Believe it. You were not meant to live forever in shock and denial, pain and guilt, anger, bargaining, depression and loneliness.

Allow yourself to embrace the "upward turn."

"In My Heart There Rings a Melody" by Elton M. Roth, 1924

DAY 30

THE SIXTH STAGE OF GRIEF
RECONSTRUCTION AND WORKING THROUGH

We will not neglect the house of our God.
Nehemiah 10: 39

Your whole being seemed to fall into the pit of despair when your grief started. However, through each stage, you have had one goal: to rebuild the walls of your life. Through each of the previous stages, you were gathering the bricks and mixing the mortar. When this stage comes along, you are finally ready to rebuild.

Nehemiah grieved because the walls of his beloved Jerusalem had been torn down. He was determined to rebuild. It was not easy. Forces came against him, tried to discourage him and fought with his idea. He planned a strategy for victory: *prayer and encouragement.* Armed with those tools, victory came, and the wall was built in 52 days! You will not rebuild your walls in that short amount of time, but you can learn from Nehemiah's perseverance. You will rebuild. With God's help, you will!

You will reconstruct the person you used to be, and in its place will be a stronger, more courageous you. You are able to do this because you desire victory over weakness. If you allow the Lord God to guide your reconstruction efforts, you will be amazed at the new you. However, this is your choice. He chooses never to violate His gift of free will by forcing your choices.

As you work with God to reconstruct your life and work through the grief process, you will begin to like yourself better. There are unnoticed gifts in all of us just waiting to be discovered. Perhaps they were not discovered earlier because you did not need those gifts. Now, you do.

When you get to this stage, every day will bring new possibilities, even though---because we understand the ups and downs of the grief process—some of the earlier stages scream to come back.

Don't doubt that you are finally here. You won't want to allow those old tapes of pain to take over. You are reconstructing and working through all the fallout from the old walls of your life. This is a new beginning.

After Nehemiah had the wall rebuilt, these words were proclaimed: "We will not neglect the house of our God." That's you. You're God's house, God's Temple. If you are a believer, He lives inside of you. Ask Him for strength and purpose so that you won't give up or neglect God's Home. You are on your way now. It really is going to get better.

DAY 31

THE LAST STAGE OF GRIEF
ACCEPTANCE AND HOPE

When doubts filled my mind, your comfort
gave me renewed hope and cheer.
Psalm 94:19

You are surprised when this last stage begins to fill your heart. Acceptance seemed so far away just a few months ago. Acceptance does not mean agreeing with what has happened. Acceptance is finally rounding the corner from the daily turmoil and struggle that says, "It cannot be! It just cannot be!" Now, you know that it can be. It has been. It always will be. It is. You stop fighting reality.

Acceptance carries within a seed of hope. Strange as it may be that the two go together, they somehow actually do. Once acceptance comes, you will not be listening for those familiar sounds and those familiar voices. Well, maybe every now and then you will. For the most part, however, you will be free from the "What if?" "How come?" and "Why me?" You will not understand anything now anymore than you understood it when it first happened, but God's grace has found a new meaning for you, and you rely on it daily. Truly, His grace has carried you through.

The psalmist reminds us in today's Scripture that as soon as doubts enter your mind, God's comfort comes to renew your hope and give you peace. As long as we look to the negatives of our lives, the overwhelming pain will always be just that: overwhelming. Your inner pain must be released daily to the only One who can cure you. Your Messiah. Jesus, the Holy One of God.

When you reach this last stage, will your days of grief finally be over? Well, not over, but much better. I believe we grieve all of our lives for those we love and lose, but the grief moves from unbearable to bearable, from tormenting to restful, from hopeless to hope.

Now, that we've gone over the stages of grief, please join me as we delve into other avenues of concern you might be feeling. Jesus is your only help. Trust Him as we continue this journey.

DAY 32

UNFINISHED BUSINESS

Don't let the sun go down while you are still angry,
for anger gives a foothold to the devil.
Ephesians 4:26-27

You never had a chance to tell her off, win that argument, or tell him what
you really thought of the way he mistreated you. When he was alive, he
kept you at bay through his own anger. You were afraid. "Someday," you
thought, "he will know how I feel about him!"

Death came before that day, and now you are in a dilemma. Family
and friends are coming up to you and expressing their sorrow for you.
You want to scream, "He wasn't that perfect! You don't know what I went
through!"

You decide to play the part until all the people go home. Then, you will
figure out what to do with your feelings. You know that you can never let
others know how he really was, the secret sins that only you knew about,
those sins you covered up for him. He was respected in the community.
No one can ever know.

Two contrasting feelings intermingle inside your heart. Your anger
toward him, and your guilt for feeling this way.

It is doubtful that anyone dies with a slate as clean and white as we
would hope. If possible, the things you know will be best kept inside. Why
hurt the children? Why disappoint his business associates? Unless you are
dealing with a matter of morality that needs to be discussed, maybe you
can keep this between you and God.

Ask yourself, "What good could this do? He is not here to defend himself. It's my word against ... my word. What would talking about it accomplish?"

But, you *can* talk about it with an ear that is safe ... the ear of Jesus. Tell Him how you feel. Cry and let out your anger to Him. Do something that helps you relieve tension ... ride a bike, take a walk, go for a swim. Determine not to let your anger give Satan a foothold in your life. Ask yourself this question: "Will I be a better person if I release this information? Will this information help anyone else?"

Sit quietly with your Lord and don't hold anything back from Him. You will be surprised how much better you feel after you've talked it over with Jesus.

DAY 33

RESCUED FROM RESENTMENT

The Lord is close to the brokenhearted; he rescues those
whose spirits are crushed. The righteous person faces many
troubles, but the Lord comes to the rescue each time.
Psalm 34: 18-19

Perhaps you are dealing with more than just your grief over your loved one's death. You are dealing with a terrifying resentment toward him/her. You gave up your life to take care of this one you loved. You sacrificed. You grew so tired from the constant day in and day out pressure. You did not want anyone else to be the caretaker. However, you needed relief. You so much wanted someone to walk in your home and insist you go out for dinner with a good friend. Yes, he was losing the battle to live, but so were you. Often, you climbed into a spot where you could cry. Deep down, in a place you don't like to go, you even resented that your life was stolen from you.

You are completely normal to struggle with having to change your life's plans in order to take care of someone else. You fit into the category of "sane," "normal," and "healthy," when you allow yourself to experience issues over the demands placed upon you. However, you don't want to stay inside of those feelings forever, because resentment will build, and you will experience a new grief that buries itself in the folds of your heart.

You are experiencing a crushed spirit. You had to give up fighting for normalcy, and you were too responsible not to be the care taker. You felt it was unfair to ask someone to do what you had to do. Your respect for your loved one cushioned his illness, and truthfully, you would have had it no other way. You lost sleep, weight and put your needs on hold. You hope no one ever saw that there was even a tad of resentment.

The above Scripture speaks to those who are brokenhearted. He reminds us that only He can rescue those whose spirits are crushed. Day after day at the same job, taking care of his personal needs, preparing his meals, feeding him, and trying to communicate with him have left you exhausted and weary. While all of the attention was on him, as well it should be, you would have loved for just one person to realize how tired you had become.

The word for this day is "rescue." Only God can do this for you. Admit your weakness (Betcha He already knows!) and ask Him to rescue you from resentment. Of course, you must do this if you wish to live in victory. Even though your feelings are normal, and you are quite sane, you will not stay this way if resentment continues to eat a hole in your heart. Talk to Jesus about this. He will surprise you with His ability to rescue you!!

DAY 34

SILENT SCREAMS

Cast all your anxiety on Him because He cares for you.
1 Peter 5:7

When Roy and I heard the news, "Frankly, Mr. Funk, there is no cure for your type of leukemia," we felt as if we had been hit by a truck. Neither of us could speak. As I drove us home from Emory University in Atlanta, the words stuck in my throat. Roy and I were silent, but I was screaming inside. A recent test at Emory was to be our answer. Ninety nine percent of those tested would be able to take a medication that was highly effective. We walked into the doctor's office sure that the news would be good, sure that Roy was in that ninety nine percent. After all, what were the odds? However, he was not. Roy was in the one percent. There was no place in my soul I could put those hurtful words. I was completely unprepared.

I don't have the words to describe how I felt on the long drive home on Interstate 75. Words like hopeless, disappointed, frustrated, and hurt don't even touch my feelings. Before we left for Emory, a dear friend said to me, "Concentrate on Jesus." I welcomed that thought, but was so optimistic about the 99% test that I dropped that thought in the backseat of my heart. After about an hour of silence, my friend's words fell on me: *Concentrate on Jesus.*

Her words were life-giving. I began to think of Jesus, how much He loved Roy, what He had done for both of us in our lives, and how much we had always depended on Him. This was no different. In fact, if we ever needed to depend on Jesus, it was now. Just as I could not find words to describe my hopeless state, I cannot seem to find the words that show what this one thought did for me. As I concentrated on Jesus, the sadness lifted. The fear subsided. Peace invaded my heart.

Something was happening to Roy, also, for soon he suggested we stop for supper at a Cracker Barrel. An unbelievable miracle occurred. We sat down to eat. We smiled. We talked. We found life again. I am still amazed. Still amazed.

I have never before or since felt such immediate release when I crawled inside a Bible verse and soaked in its meaning. "Cast all your anxiety upon Him for He cares for you." This Scripture came to life that day.

If necessary, write this Scripture on index cards, and tape it all over your home. Remind yourself that there is life in the living Word of our living Lord!! It works. It really does work!

DAY 35

FINDING HOPE

Brothers, we do not want you to be ignorant about those who fall
asleep, or to grieve like the rest of men, who have no hope.
1 Thessalonians 4:13

The phrase, "those who fall asleep," refers to those who die. Roy and
I were now at the place where the realization of death fell on us every
day. However, Paul tells us in the above verse that believers are not to be
ignorant about death and are not to grieve like those who have no hope. It
does not mean that we cannot grieve. It just means we grieve, but we have
hope. We know about heaven. We have *glorious* hope.

That did not ease, however, the pain of watching my husband lose
energy and weight, the pain of watching my loved one die. As his body
showed signs of dying, I felt I, too, was dying. I had no good response the
day Roy looked at me and made a simple statement, not in anger, but in
fact. "I used to be able to walk long distances and move heavy furniture.
I cannot do any of that now."

I made a list of things that hope *could not* do for me. (1) Hope could
not change the circumstances. (2) Hope could not make Roy well (3)
Hope could not go against the ultimate will of God (4) Hope could not
suddenly bring a miracle drug into Roy's life, and (4) Hope would not
take away reality.

Then, I made a list of what hope *can* do for me. (1) Hope reminds
me that death is not the end for Roy (2) Hope reminds me that I will see
him again one day (3) Hope tells me that I still have responsibilities and
obligations to my work and to others, and these responsibilities will give

me energy as I grieve, (4) Jesus and Hope are synonymous. If I know Jesus, then I know Hope. (5) Concentrating on Jesus is the only real hope I have.

The healing balm of the gospel of Jesus Christ is a mystery. I can look all through the dictionary and never find words to tell you how this happens in actuality ... how hope sifted into my life in beautiful, non-tangible ways. But, it did.

Jesus is the only answer for your hopelessness. Trust Him, even when you don't understand.

Trust Him, especially when you don't understand.

DAY 36

JUST WHO DO WE THINK WE ARE?

Have you ever given orders to the morning, or shown the dawn its place?
Job 38: 12

Job had an arsenal of questions about why these terrible things were happening to him. Read Job chapter 38, and you will learn that God never answered any of his questions. Instead, God pointed out His divine hand in the order of the universe, with the assumption being that Job could not possibly understand the mind of God. Who did Job think he was, anyway, to question God's purposes in Job's difficulties?

Hard as it is for us to read this, there is a truth hidden in the book of Job: *God is God, and we are not.* No matter how hard we fight, baulk, plead, beg, argue, cry, scream or fuss, in the end we are not privy to certain things. On the way home from the doctor's office, Roy said to me, "At the end of the day, God owes me nothing."

But, I wanted God to owe Roy something. Roy was a tither, never missed church, taught Sunday School and sang in the choir. He was honest. He gave to those in need. He was the best steward of the Lord's money I have ever known.

Yet, in truth, God owed Roy nothing. Matthew 5:45 speaks loudly on this subject when Jesus says, "He causes his sun to rise on the evil and the good, and sends rain on the righteous and the unrighteous."

Roy had lived a righteous life, and yet God's ultimate plan is that the murderer and Roy are no different where this is concerned. God is God, and He chooses to send rain on those living in obvious rebellion of His love, as well as on those who have lived their lives for Him. I often wondered why leukemia did not claim a perpetual child abuser instead of my Roy. I soon realized I would live in the depths of pain and rebellion if I stayed in that state of mind. After all, who do I think I am? I have never given orders to the morning, or shown the dawn its place. I am teeny-tiny in the great scheme of life.

You and I can either accept Matthew 5:45, recognizing the unbelievable and seemingly unfair kindness of God to everyone, or we can rebel and become bitter, lonely, and disgusting to be around.

I will never understand why Roy had to die, but I will always understand that God loved Roy by allowing Him into His kingdom on earth and in heaven. If I *get that,* all other questions seem small.

DAY 37

FIGHTING THE ENEMY

Be self-controlled and alert. Your enemy the devil prowls around
like a roaring lion looking for someone to devour. Resist him …
1 Peter 5: 8-9a

Satan loves to get right in the middle of your pain and whisper things in
your ears to take your eyes off of Jesus. "You've tried to do everything right.
Why is God allowing this pain in your life?" or "If you really believed, she
would be healed." or "Do you remember that day in Junior High? God is
punishing you for that."

So, it's important to keep in the Word of God so that you can separate
the truth from Satan's lies. After all, he is the father of lies. (John 8:44)
Jesus warned us against following Satan, a roaring, devouring lion from
the beginning, with no truth in him.

But, we are good church goers! Does Jesus seriously think we might
fall prey to the lies of Satan? Absolutely. We are the most vulnerable of all
because we *think we are immune.* We who have accepted Jesus as our Savior
and are working out our salvation through sanctification … yes, us … .we
are the most vulnerable to the lies of Satan. Those living in constant sin
and unrighteousness don't have a clue that there is a better way. So, tell me.
If you were Satan would you even bother with them? They are already his.
Satan's concentration is on those who belong to the Lord. He is constantly
trying to get you to come over to his side.

Don't believe him! That sin from twenty five years ago … was bought
and paid for with the blood of Jesus. Accept God's forgiveness. You are
not receiving punishment for what you did then or now. Christians who

are bent over from a load of past guilt have not yet completely received the mercy, grace and forgiveness of our wonderful Father God. Satan is the father of lies. God is the Father of Love, Mercy and Grace.

Let it go. Receive anew God's love for you. Some of the most beautiful words in the Bible … and so many of them actually win that honor … come from James 4:7-8: "Submit yourselves, then, to God. Resist the devil, and he will flee from you. Come near to God and he will come near to you."

This almost sounds too simple to be true, yet it takes focus. Here are the steps. (1) Submit to God, (2) Resist the devil (3) Come near to God (4) He will come near to you.

I love the truth of this verse. If I come near to God, then he is certainly not going to turn away from me. He is going to come near to me. Get a picture in your mind of you coming toward God. He sees you, and comes toward you! Hebrews 13:5 reminds us that God has said, "Never will I leave you; never will I forsake you."

So, tell Satan to just take a hike. You have better things to do today than to listen to his lies!

DAY 38

IF I AM A CHRISTIAN, THEN WHY AM I AFRAID?

The Lord is with me; I will not be afraid. What can man do to me?
Psalm 118: 6

Fears jump in and out of our thoughts, preying on our vulnerability. Negative thoughts hammer us, when what we really need is *strength* to face another day. Questions jump in and out of our minds: *How do I get through this? Will I be able to face each day without him/her? I am not used to this kind of responsibility. Who will I call when I cannot take care of those things I am not accustomed to handling?*

God knows all about your needs and your fears, and the psalmist quotes your heart when he asks the question, "What can man do to me?" That question is preceded by the unfailing truth that God is with you, so you need not be afraid. You can repeat that verse often during the day, discovering that those words have meat in them. They are not milk for babies. They are the solid steak for grown-ups. Solid meat gives you strength.

Your fear may revolve around finances, your business, discontentment with friends or family or just anything that Satan wants to use to scare you. Be prepared that some days will simply begin and end with those questions not answered. As you rely on God and on Godly influences in your life, allow God the benefit of your doubt. Give Him time. Trust

Him. Believe, and take ownership in these words, "What can man do to me?"

Nothing is happening to you that has caught God unaware. He knows all about it. So, sit down with your coffee and your Bible, slow down your racing mind, and let God soothe you.

DAY 39

LIVING ROOM SERMON

Your Will Be Done
Matthew 6:10

I never wanted to believe that it was actually God's will to take Roy from me. Deep in my heart, I lived in a world of make-believe. Surely, this was all a bad dream.

Then, I heard the best sermon I have ever heard. It was in my living room. It was eight words long, and was delivered by my husband as he sat in his recliner.

Roy's daddy had come from Michigan for a visit. He felt the Lord wanted him to anoint his son with oil and pray for him. Janet, Roy's sister, and I stood by as we listened to Mr. Funk. First, he placed his 93 year old worn-out-from-a-life-of-farming finger into the oil. Then, he made a cross on Roy's forehead and uttered this simple prayer.

"God, this is my only son. He's sick. He represents the seventh generation of our family to serve you. I am asking you to heal him."

That was it. No loud demands. No reminders that perhaps there was more for Roy to do on this earth. Nothing. Simple and to the point.

When he finished, he said to us, "Now I've done what He told me to do. What He does is up to Him."

Then, these words from Roy: "And whatever He does will be okay."

I was speechless. Through months of dealing with sickness, Roy had come to the conclusion that his healing was not up to the medical profession or even necessarily to a supernatural intervention. Ultimately, his healing was up to God. And whichever way God decided to work, Roy was all right with that. He would either be healed on earth or healed in heaven. Either way, Roy would win.

That day, my husband taught me how to die with victory. His eight-word sentence ... the best sermon I have ever heard ... rings often in my heart. It helps me make it through the days without Roy. Roy accepted his death. I had to, also.

DAY 40

CHOOSING TO BE CHEERFUL

A cheerful heart is good medicine, but a
crushed spirit dries up the bones.
Proverbs 17: 22

I did not want dry bones, as the above Proverb states. I wanted life in my bones, so I had to make a choice to be cheerful. After all, who wants to be around a sour woman? I remember as a child, my mother quoted this verse, a bit differently from her Bible than I read it today in mine. "Laughter doeth good, like medicine" she would say.

It's true. How long has it been since you have laughed? How long has it been since you have allowed the healing oil of laughter to tickle every bone and muscle in your body? I truly believe a happy heart has a healing effect on our bodies.

For me, watching Carol Burnette, The Andy Griffith Show, and the Dick Van Dyke reruns brought laughter to my heart and healing to my bones. I also am very fortunate to have some wonderfully funny friends who can make me go into a loud giggle with their wit. I try to be around them as often as possible.

You might be afraid to laugh, thinking that others will interpret your laughter as disrespectful during your grieving period. Let that go. Choose to let laughter be part of your medicine as you heal. You need to laugh.

Proverbs 14:13 reminds us that "Even in laughter, the heart may ache." I take that to mean that my heart-aches remain even as I laugh, but I accept that God gave me laughter to be a medicine for those deep aches. It's working for me.

Give yourself permission to laugh every day about something. You will be surprised how much laughter helps.

DAY 41

GOD DELIGHTS, HE LOVES, AND HE SINGS

He will take great delight in you. He will quiet you with
His love. He will rejoice over you with singing.
Zephaniah 3: 17b

What is God doing while you are complaining, fussing, demanding, and arguing with Him over what has happened to you? Does He sit down on His throne, throw His hands up in the air and declare that He just cannot do one thing with you? Does He mope around because you are disappointed in Him? Does He get frustrated with you? Actually, He does none of the above.

Zephaniah has a great verse that explains perfectly the way your Father feels about you. Just as your children have often delighted you, so *you* delight the heart of God. His love can quiet you. He sings over you as He rejoices simply because you are His child! He is not expecting you to be perfect. He loves you and puts no condition on His love. He loves you when you are in a good mood and when you are in a bad one. He loves you when you are smiling and when you are crying. Before you were even born, He made a decision to love you. That will never change.

I have never heard God sing, but I believe I hear His song each time I hear a beautiful Christian melody sung by one in whom He has placed the gift of music. Certain artist's songs reached out to me after Roy's death, and perhaps you have found your favorites, too, as you stepped into grief. Accept those songs and beautiful voices as being straight from the Father's heart to you. Get so close to Him that you can feel His arms around you, quieting you with His love. Imagine Him rejoicing over you with singing.

What a beautiful word picture of the Father's heart. Can you hear Him singing over you?

DAY 42

WONDER WHY I NEVER HEARD FROM HER?

Restore to Me the Joy of your salvation and grant
me a willing spirit, to sustain me.
Psalm 51:12

Get ready for this. You just might easily get hurt during your initial grieving period. Life will be moving at a fast pace as you make funeral arrangements and greet your family and friends. One day you will suddenly stop and realize that you have never heard from a certain friend. Self-pity wants to sit on your doorsteps as you assess who has not contacted you. I don't believe God feels like singing over us at this time, but I do believe He keeps His song going, perhaps with a softer sound.

Have you stopped to think that this person might (1) not know what to say, (2) be going through her own difficulties, (3) have actually sent a card, and it got lost in the mail, or (4) have let so much time pass after your loved one's death that she is ashamed to get in touch with you now?

Let's look at each of these, with our minds turned to giving everybody the benefit of the doubt. This is no time for self-pity to become your best friend. Self-pity is cunning, dangerous and is up to no good! It will only interfere with what God is trying to do in your life.

(1) She does not know what to say. This is universal. Many people shy away from someone's pain because they feel they don't have the right words. You, however, have learned that simply their being in your presence brings relief, even if they don't utter a word. Forgive them. It's not worth the energy you are spending on this. (2) She might be going through her own difficulties. Let go of the thought that no matter if she is not, it's not

as bad as what you have faced. You don't know what is happening in her life. Forgive her. Pray for whatever is hurting her. (3) She might have sent a card and it got lost in the mail. It *could* happen. Fretting over this is not worth the turmoil you put yourself in because they have not sent a card or called you. Choose to forgive instead of to fret. (4) So, she has been busy. That's not worth losing a friend. Love her anyway. Forgive her. You will be the winner even if you never hear from her again.

Ask the Lord to restore to you any joy that you have lost worrying over these non-essential items in your life. Decide what is important and what is not. Let it go. You will find immeasurable happiness in being able to forgive someone.

DAY 43

TOUCHING HEAVEN IN A DREAM

… An angel of the Lord appeared to Joseph in a dream. "Get
up and take the child and his mother to Egypt. Stay there until I
tell you for Herod is going to search for the child to kill him."
Matthew 2:13

Joseph had the care of baby Jesus and Mary. He had to be warned about
Herod. God chose to give that warning in a dream. The dream was
specific. An angel appeared and said (1) Get up, (2) Take the child and his
mother to Egypt and (3) stay there until you hear from me.

I have had two dreams about Roy since he left for heaven. One was
just a picture of him in our bedroom, standing close to my side of the bed.
Nothing was said. That was nice, but the other one gave me great peace.

We were on our way to church. Roy was driving, and he was dressed in
a suit, looking so handsome and about twenty years younger than he was
when he died. I was in the back seat, leaning up to ask him a question. He
said, "You know? When I decided to leave, I went fast."

It was Roy's voice. It was him, thinking things through the way he
always did. It was him, settling things in his mind about his death. Always
a deep thinker, Roy was just being Roy.

It was true. Once the Oncology department told us there was nothing
more they could do, and they were putting Roy on hospice … things
moved quickly. Roy went to heaven in just three days. So, the dream was an
accurate portrayal of what actually happened. However, I had a question
to ask him, and the dream ended before I had that chance.

I wanted to make sure I had done everything necessary to make his Home-going and last days on earth as easy as they could be. I leaned up from the back seat to ask, "Roy, could I have done anything to make your last days easier?" when suddenly the dream ended. Surprisingly, I did not feel cheated. In truth, I knew I had done all I could do. I suppose that line of questioning is normal.

I realize it was only a dream, but I truly felt I had been visiting with Roy. I awoke from that dream refreshed and thankful for the chance to be with him once again. It was very real. In a way I can't explain, I felt I had touched heaven in a dream. I don't expect I will have that opportunity to be with Roy this way very often, maybe never again.

After my mother's mother had been in heaven around thirty years, my mama saw her in a dream. She asked her, "Mama I've missed you! Where have you been?"

Her mother answered, "I've been in a beautiful garden."

That was it, and as far as I know, she never dreamed of her mother again. She already knew where her mother was. She was assured, however, in this dream.

God is good. I love His unexpected surprises.

DAY 44

JESUS, YOU ARE THE ONE I LIKE TO BE WITH BEST

One thing I ask of the Lord, this is what I seek; that
I may dwell in the house of the Lord all the days of
my life, to gaze upon the beauty of the Lord
Psalm 27:4

When you finally settle down and have time to think about all that has been happening in your life, you will draw a line through the unimportant and a line under the important! What deserves your time and energy? Underline it. What needs to be thrown out of your thinking? Strike through it!

These things have to be conscious choices, for it is all too easy to give way to petty thinking. In today's verse, the psalmist speaks of one thing that he desires, and that is to dwell in the house of the Lord and to gaze at the beauty of the Lord.

That sort of puts things in perspective. Notice that he does not ask for healing, for wealth, for good fortune, for anything that would make his time on earth more prosperous. No, he asks to stay in the house of the Lord forever. He desires to gaze upon the beauty of the Lord every day.

Does this describe you? Are you there, yet? Is your heart's desire to see Jesus every day in everything you do? Most of us would answer, "Not there yet!"

I'm not there either. I *want* to be. I want so much to desire being with Him more than anything this earth has to offer. Often, my human heart aches for things to be the way they used to be, but there is no good thing that comes from this kind of thinking. It hurts too much.

One day, as I was summing up things in my life, perhaps feeling a bit introspective, this thought came into my mind with great clarity. "Jesus, you are the One I like to be with best." It has to be this way. I am never guaranteed anything in this world. If I dwell on what I would like to happen, disappointment can easily move into my heart. I am never guaranteed that friends will stay with me or that family will be close by. I am never guaranteed that I can pay all of my bills on time. I am never guaranteed a respite from disease.

I have only one guarantee, and you do, too. We are guaranteed that Jesus will never leave us or forsake us, that He will walk by our side through the difficulties of our lives. You might want to underline that.

Jesus, you ARE the One I like to be with best!

DAY 45

IT'S NOT ABOUT ME

But, the fruit of the Spirit is love, joy, peace, patience, kindness,
goodness, faithfulness, gentleness and self-control
Galatians 5:22

You may be crushed today as you face a new day. You might be in great
pain over your loss. You deserve time to grieve. However, grief is not a
license to take Galatians 5:22 out of your Bible. God's Spirit wants to
display fruit even in life's most difficult times. It may take a little more
time with the Lord in order for your fruit not to tarnish right now. Allow
Him to polish each part of the Spirit's fruit as you continue to heal and as
you soak in His Word.

It's not about you. Someone you loved died. Your grief is sometime
inconsolable. Ask the Lord to help you think of pain others might have.
They are hurting, too. Maybe there are sons or daughters, sisters or
brothers, parents and close friends who are struggling just as much as you
might be. It takes a great amount of grace to crawl out of your pain and
reach out to others during this time. Before you even try, take the hand of
the only One who can help you do this.

Someone told me once that death can bring on divorce. The pain is
so intense, people get hurt with each other so easily, and life sails along on
rough waters for a good while. We are extra sensitive, extra cautious about
what we say and about what others say. Wonder why it is that something
so devastating could bring on something else so devastating. Ask the Lord
to help you heal without hurting someone in the process.

"If I speak with the tongues of men and of angels and have not love, I am only a resounding gong or a clanging cymbal … if I have faith that can move mountains, but have not love, I am nothing. If I give all I possess to the poor and surrender my body to flames, but have not love, I gain nothing." (1 Corinthians 13: 1-3)

Have you felt that because you are grieving, you don't have to show love to others? Do you believe that your pain gives you license to hurt others? God has never told us that it's okay for us to be unkind when we are in pain. He has never lowered His standard of love, not for one second. He expects us to do the same.

If you are feeling an unusual amount of tenseness today, slow down, breathe deeply, sink into the Word and allow yourself to feel God's love and favor, which incidentally you do not deserve. Then, give out love and favor to those around you, who incidentally don't deserve it either.

If we counted on our degree of goodness to receive His degree of love, we would be lost forever in a never-ending sea of hopelessness. That's what's so sweet about grace.

DAY 46

NEEDING A STEADY DRIP
OF UNFAILING LOVE

Though He brings grief, He will show compassion,
so great is His unfailing love
Lamentations 3:32

When I was in the hospital, I could not go anywhere without my IV fluids going with me.

Up and down the hallway, to the end window and back, and into the bathroom. Wherever I went, my IV went with me. It was a bit cumbersome, too. The three pronged rollers at the bottom fought each other, one screaming, "Go this way," and the other fighting back, "No, go *this* way!" At least that's how it was for me. Maybe you are a better driver of an IV drip than I am.

God's love is like a constant dripping IV. It never stops. You don't even have to be stuck to get His IV of love. There is no use in us pretending that life is always a breeze, always wonderful and fair, always victorious. It simply is not. We may go through days of breeze, days of life being fair and victorious, but all of us know the depth of pain into which we can sink after we go through death. Sometimes, you might get stuck in that pit for days or weeks, thinking there is no way to climb out. The above verse can help, the emphasis being on "unfailing love."

Think of God's unfailing love being an IV drip, moving all around your home with you, out into the yard, and to the store. You cannot get away from it. The drip is constant, steady, always on time and intentional:

88

to bring you healing. No matter how much we fight it, or try to run away from it, or even resent it, God's love stays.

I struggle with the first part of that verse, "Though He bring grief …" I much more prefer the wording, "Though He allows grief," not bring, but allow. Did He know about Roy's sickness? Yes, because He knows everything. Did He actually engineer circumstances so Roy's blood would be diseased? I don't think so. I believe Roy lived, as do you and I, within the natural order of this universe which is *highly* infected with sin. What happened to him could happen to anyone who walks on this earth. My personal belief is that every time a sparrow falls, God knows about it. (Matthew 10:29) If He cares so much to notice a sparrow, then surely Roy was high up on his *Notice, Care and Compassion list.* In a way that is too far above me to explain, God knew. I even think He knew and cried. He hates what sin has done to His children.

Even if you think it is a bit corny, indulge yourself today and imagine an IV drip of God's love moving all around your home with you. Receive His love, feel His love, Imagine His love … as it moves into your vascular system and into your heart, muscles and bones. Does it get any better than this?

DAY 47

OILED, OILED, AND THEN OILED SOME MORE

Is any one of you sick? He should call the elders of the church to
pray over him and *anoint him with oil* in the name of the Lord.
And the prayer offered in faith will make the sick person well ...
James 5:14

I loved that Roy welcomed all who wanted to come anoint him with oil.
Cathy brought an anointed handkerchief. He put it under his pillow each
night. Andy and Patsy came with oil. Roy received with gratitude. Shirley
and Debbie prayed over Roy an hour, oiling his head, arms, hands and legs.
He was super lubed by the time they got finished. That wasn't all. They
sang over him. How I love each of these friends for trusting the Bible and
doing what the Word said.

It would be easy to think that God must not have been listening on
those days. After all, the church came and anointed him in the name of
the Lord, but Roy did not get well. I disagree. I saw wellness occurring
inside Roy, in the depths of his heart ... things that I am very sure were a
supernatural healing resulting from being anointed with oil. Roy softened.
He listened. He turned no one away. That would not have been the
reaction of Roy twenty or thirty years ago. Not that he did not believe
what the Word said during that time in his life. He did. *He was just not at
a point of need then.* When Jesus brought Roy to a point of great need, Roy
was open for anything and everything God might want to do. I believe
healing of emotions happened. I know forgiveness did. Roy became tender.

Not one to easily give compliments, Roy gave me the best compliment
I have ever had the day before he died. He said, "I'm very fortunate to have

had you." It was worth everything to hear that. Did he always think that about me? Well, maybe. Would he have ever told me? Well, no. He was more one to show than to tell. I had settled happily with that side of him,--because who would not appreciate a husband who did all of the cooking, all of the yard work, AND his own laundry--- but oh my, when he said those golden words to me, they sank deeply, *a well of swirling joy* swimming over my insides. What a beautiful gift he gave me before he left. Can you see why I cannot stop counting my blessings?

Will I stop anointing with oil if I am asked just because Roy did not get well? Never. In everything we do, the will of God must supersede our desires, our hopes,our wishes. It's really all up to Him. He is the designer of life, the sustainer of life, the giver and ruler of life. So, we press on, knowing that God is definitely our best and dearest friend, and that He has reasons we cannot begin to understand. It seems inconsistent to stop trusting Him just because He didn't do what I wanted.

In one of her books, the late Catherine Marshall taught me this: "I want God more than I want what I want." That has been an invaluable, necessary, and healing teaching for me.

And, I do.

DAY 48

CEMETERY VISITS

Now, this is eternal life: that they may know you, the only
true God, and Jesus Christ, whom you have sent.
John17:3

Roy is buried in our city cemetery on a street named Genesis! I think
that's fitting and just about perfect! Genesis tells of new beginnings, the
creation of the world. Death is a new beginning. I know Roy is not there,
and maybe I'm strange, but I get no particular satisfaction from going to
his grave. Even though it was the last place Roy's physical body lay, I don't
get a sense of nearness from going.

I'll tell you, though, when I do get a sense of nearness: when I think
about or read about heaven; when I stop to remind myself that if Jesus is
at the right hand of the Father in heaven, and the Holy Spirit resides in
me, then I am close ... very close ... to Roy's residence, too. Somehow,
we are connected in death through the spiritual plan God has laid out for
believers. If eternal life begins here on earth, when we accept Jesus as our
Savior, then I am living where Roy is living, inside eternal life. The big
difference, however, is that he has gone full circle.

You and I are living in eternal life *now* if we are in a personal
relationship with God through His Son, Jesus Christ. Our saved loved
ones have continued their earthly relationship of eternal life and now are
in a heavenly relationship of eternal life. Their relationship now is *up close
and personal.*

It would be wonderful if God chose to let those of us on earth speak to
those in heaven. However, God is wise not to allow this, not only for the

sake of those of us still living, but for the sake of His heavenly church. Why would He permit them to listen to our hurting hearts? Would a loving God allow them to hear our cries of how much we miss and love them? They are in *heaven*. They are free from earth's limitations. They don't think or reason the way earth-folks do.

What would I say? "Roy, I miss you." How would he answer?

"What does 'miss you' mean?"

In the Old Testament a thick curtain hung in front of The Most Holy Place. It was reserved by God Himself, entered into only once a year, on the Day of Atonement, by the High Priest who went for the purpose of bringing a sacrifice for the forgiveness of the sins of the people. When Jesus died, that curtain ripped in two, signifying that the death of Jesus paved the way for mere man to enter into that room. Our High Priest, Jesus, made it possible through His death for each of us to talk to God directly.

I'm telling you … that's shouting news!!

Similarly, there is an imaginary thick curtain that separates us now from heaven, that Most Holy Place where God dwells. Believers will go there to live, but only when God, through His sovereign plan, splits that curtain and brings our spirits there when we die.

A man named Jim Hill wrote, "Oh what a day that will be, when my Jesus I shall see; And I'll look upon His face, the One who saved me by His grace; When He takes me by the hand, and leads me to the promised land, what a day, glorious day, that will be!"

Eternal life!! God's perfect gift of grace and love to His children!

DAY 49

TRUSTING GOD IN THE UNEXPLAINABLE

And we know that in all things God works for the good of those
who love Him, who have been called according to His purpose.
Romans 8: 28

If it is true that *fools rush in where angels fear to tread,* then I would be indeed foolish to even try to explain why things happen as they do. If I wanted to attempt that impossible task, I would end up closing my computer and my Bible, and spending the rest of my life in confusion.

These devotionals are not meant to explain God's actions in the death of one we have loved. They are meant *to help the suffering, to bring comfort to the hopeless,* and *to remind all of us that God was not asleep when that unbearable pain entered your life.* The answers to your pain lie within the pages of your Bible, in the comfort of a kind, listening friend, in the tears you are shedding, in beautiful and intimate times of prayer, and in the hope that comes through Jesus Christ! There is no other way to face tragedy. Grief may cause you to run around in circles, make wrong decisions, choose wrong actions and wrong friends for years until you come back to the realization that none of these things can make a *lasting* difference in your life.

People will want to be there for you, but after a while, they will get tired of your self-emphasis. Your daily plunge into self-pity will cause even the closest of friends to grow weary. Give yourself the proper time you need to grieve; but allow yourself to grieve with your heart set always toward eventual healing.

As I have been writing these devotionals, I am aware that I face death through limited vision. My mother, daddy, mother-in-law and husband are in heaven. They all arrived there through either a stroke, old age or cancer. In all of these cases, I had time to prepare myself for their passing. I have no experience, as some of you do, with a sudden call in the night with news of a murder, suicide, or a terrible vehicle accident. I know nothing firsthand of the worst death of all, losing a child.

What I do know for sure is that we all need each other. None of us can face such life-altering circumstances as the loss of a loved one by ourselves. I hope you will accept the kindness and empathy of others, knowing they may not know what to say, but at least they show up. That's what we want when death hits. We want others to show up--- not to tell us what to do, how to behave or even that they understand. We just want somebody to show up. If that has not happened for you, make it your goal ... that you will just *show up* for someone else when they face grief. They will be so glad you did, and believe it or not, your *showing up* for them may even be another part of your own healing.

This verse in Romans is one of my favorites. God is behind the scenes of what you cannot see. He is working things out for your good. He may not tell you what to do or how to behave. But, He will show up. You can count on that.

DAY 50

BREAK THROUGH

The Lord gave and the Lord has taken away; May the
Name of the Lord be Praised In all of this, Job did
not sin by charging God with wrongdoing
Job1: 21b& 2

You might look at the above verse and think you are wrong not to be
praising God because someone has been taken from you. That is *not* what
these verses indicate. Read it like this: "The Lord gave and the Lord has
taken away; May the Name of the Lord be praised *anyway*."

At this time, Job, who was a model of trust and obedience to God,
had lost his family and his possessions. In a dialogue with Satan, God had
given Satan permission to strike everything—except Job's life. Satan had
a plan. *Satan wanted to prove that Job would eventually curse God, and that
Job worshiped God, not out of love, but because God had given him so much.*
That sheds a different light on the book of Job and on this Scripture in
particular.

Job was a man who loved and enjoyed a good life. He never blamed
God that everything was eventually taken away from him. Job did not
understand, but he proclaimed the goodness and faithfulness of his God,
no matter what. He recognized that we all live in a fallen world, where
good people and bad people alike are hit with the consequences of sin.
Because of his faithfulness to God, Job's life ended with great blessings.
In fact, "The Lord blessed the latter part of Job's life more than the first."
(Job 42:12)

You will receive a break-through in your pain when you accept that God is not trying to hurt you, blame you, punish you or deprive you because of your loss. He is a good God, loving you and hurting with you. He is a kind Father, desiring that you come to Him for comfort. Whatever else we may not understand about death, we are to gain this clear understanding from our loss: God's love remains. He never leaves. He cares. He wants to help you.

You will close this devotional book and still have many questions. So do I. But, I know that my Redeemer lives, and I know that my Lord loves me and cares about me. I know that He shows up and He stays. I think I can make it if I keep those thoughts foremost in my heart every day.

I believe you can, too. May the Lord bless you and keep you!